ONE GOD · ONE WORLD · ONE CHURCH
ONE VISION

ONE GOD · ONE WORLD · ONE CHURCH

ONE VISION

KENNETH F. HANEY

GENERAL SUPERINTENDENT
UNITED PENTECOSTAL CHURCH INTERNATIONAL

One God, One World, One Church, One Vision

by Kenneth F. Haney

Copyright ©2001 United Pentecostal Church International
Hazelwood, MO 63042-2299

Cover design by Paul Povolni

ISBN 0-7577-2190-7

Unless otherwise indicated, all quotations of Scripture are from The King James Version of the Bible.

Printed in the United States of America

Printed by

WORD AFLAME®PRESS
8855 DUNN ROAD
HAZELWOOD, MO 63042-2299

CONTENTS

DEDICATION

This book is dedicated to the faithful leadership of the United Pentecostal Church International, which includes the General Board, the division heads, which are the elected officials, and those working in leadership positions within each division. It is dedicated also to the many faithful employees at the World Evangelism Center. For we together are committed to the fulfillment of the Great Commission!

FOREWORD

What an exciting and eventful time for truth to be proclaimed! The Twentieth Century history of the church reveals some beautiful and dramatic times. The formation and birth of a movement that God ordained to come into existence for this latter time, for the gospel must reach every nation—all people. Truth must triumph!

Satan has held the world captive long enough. Please understand that we have been commissioned through prophecy. It is a special mission. In the Book of Revelation concerning the seven letters to the seven churches, prophetically the sixth church is *where* we are and *who* we are.

Jesus said, "I know thy works: behold, I HAVE SET BEFORE THEE AN OPEN DOOR, and no man can shut it: for thou hast a little strength, and hast kept my word, and hast not denied my name" (Revelation 3:8).

We have been given an open door to evangelize the world with the truth of salvation. We must not fail to step through that door! As a movement we have been brought to the kingdom for such a time as this. It is essential that we tell the world that Jesus is God!

Through revelation He will reveal His name. God is going to bring His church to the forefront as vessels of truth to be mightily used in this final thrust. This will include the people that have been faithful to the revelation of the name, who have exalted that name by proclaiming baptism in that name, who have been targeted throughout the religious world as One God or Oneness people, who have taught and preached that Jesus is God! This cannot be delegated to a few, or even to 50%, 60% or 80%, but every pastor and minister must buy into this mission and from there it must filter down to every saint.

Yes, it is ONE GOD, ONE CHURCH, for ONE WORLD; may we all catch the ONE VISION for the final thrust!

PREFACE

The Lord impressed me with the story of Nehemiah in relation to the "quick" work that is needed to be done in these last days by the United Pentecostal Church International.

The need of the hour is for the ministry to unite ourselves as ONE CHURCH to reach ONE WORLD with ONE MESSAGE that JESUS IS THE ONLY GOD! This is the vision that must be done quickly.

Nehemiah was carried away into captivity as a boy under Persian rule. It was highly unlikely that a Hebrew slave would ever rise to any position of prominence. But the hand of God was upon him and he succeeded in becoming cup-bearer to King Artaxerxes, which meant that he had daily contact with the king and lived in the palace.

One day Nehemiah had a visit from a distant kin, Hanani, who was from the old country. Hanani shared with Nehemiah the deplorable state of Jerusalem, how that the majestic walls of the Holy City had been brought to ruin and the gates of entrance burned by fire. The result of such conditions made it possible for the enemy to intrude and abuse the Jewish people of the city.

After the departure of Hanani, Nehemiah reflected upon his memory of a better day and of the magnificent walls that had now been brought to ruin. His vision of his childhood and now this disturbing report brought great consternation to the heart of Nehemiah.

Nehemiah 1:4 states: "And it came to pass, when I heard these words, that I sat down and wept, and mourned certain days, and fasted, and prayed before the God of heaven." Nehemiah wept, mourned, fasted and prayed certain days before God. His emotions were stirred. Before a people can perform a great work in the kingdom of God there must be a stirring of the emotions, a passion which brings us to a dependency upon God. As Nehemiah wept, fasted, and prayed, so must we. Nehemiah prayed the following prayer, which demonstrates his humility:

"Let thine ear now be attentive,
and thine eyes open, that thou mayest
hear the prayer of thy servant, which I
pray before thee now, day and night, for the
children of Israel thy servants, and confess
the sins of the children of Israel, which we
have sinned against thee: both I and my
father's house have sinned. We have dealt
very corruptly against thee, and have not
kept the commandments, nor the statutes,
nor the judgments, which thou commandedst
thy servant Moses. O LORD, I beseech thee, let
now thine ear be attentive to the prayer of
thy servant, and to the prayer of thy
servants, who desire to fear thy name: and
prosper, I pray thee, thy servant this
day, and grant him mercy
in the sight of this man."
Nehemiah 1:6-7, 11

He was not arrogant and self-satisfied but felt his need of God for himself and his people. All prayer and fasting must terminate in a purpose. Thus it was so with Nehemiah's time of prayer and fasting.

The next day when Nehemiah went before King Artaxerxes, the king asked, "Why is thy countenance sad?" (God was preparing the heart of the king after Nehemiah's time of prayer and fasting. Before the accomplishment of any great mission, there must be prayer and fasting and seeking after God.)

Nehemiah answered the king: "And said unto the king, Let the king live for ever: why should not my countenance be sad, when the city, the place of my fathers' sepulchres, lieth waste, and the gates thereof are consumed with fire?" (Nehemiah 2:3).

Then the king asked the question, "What is thy request?" Nehemiah was ready with his answer: "If I have found favor in thy sight I pray that thou wouldst send me that I may build it."

God touched the heart of the king; for the king to grant permission to Nehemiah to go could only have been an act of God. For the king to send him to rebuild the walls meant that Nehemiah was going in the king's authority and with his blessing, which in reality would mean that he was commissioned to perform a duty.

The king also gave him letters of authorization to the governors to cut down cedars to rebuild the gates:

"Moreover I said unto the king, If it
please the king, let letters be given me to the
governors beyond the river, that they may
convey me over till I come into Judah; and a
letter unto Asaph the keeper of the king's

forest, that he may give me timber to make
beams for the gates of the palace which
appertained to the house, and for the wall of
the city, and for the house that I shall enter
into. And the king granted me, according to
the good hand of my God upon me. Then I
came to the governors beyond the river,
and gave them the king's letters."
Nehemiah 2:7-9

Nehemiah, stirred by God, prayed and fasted; then he asked for what he needed to do the job, and God gave him what he asked for by the hand of the highest authority on earth: the King. When God stirs us up to do a job, we must not be afraid to ask for that which we need, for Jesus said, "Ask, and it shall be given you" (Matthew 7:7).

Not only did the king send him with letters of authorization, but also sent an emissary with Nehemiah. "Now the king had sent captains of the army and horsemen with me" (Nehemiah 2:9).

God will never call a man or send a man without equipping him to do the work. Therefore, God will equip the church for the latter-day harvest. Even though there will be obstacles to overcome, God's equipping will be sufficient.

Before Nehemiah spoke to the children of Israel, he surveyed the situation: "And I arose in the night, I and some few men with me; neither told I any man what my God had put in my heart to do at Jerusalem: . . . And I went out by night . . . and viewed the walls of Jerusalem, which were broken down, and the gates thereof were consumed with fire" (Nehemiah 2:12-14).

Then he called the people together and said, "Ye see the distress that we are in, how Jerusalem lieth waste, and the gates thereof are burned with fire: come, and let us build up the wall of Jerusalem, that we be no more a reproach" (Nehemiah 2:17). *"Come let us build up the walls!"* was his battle cry.

And the people said, "Let us rise up and build. So they strengthened their hands for this good work" (Nehemiah 2:18). THEY STRENGTHENED THEIR HANDS TO BUILD.

When the enemy, Sanballat and Tobiah, the Arabians, and the Ammonites, and the Ashdodites heard of his mission, it grieved them exceedingly that there was coming a man to seek the welfare of Israel (Nehemiah 4:7).

Not only were they angry, but they also conspired together to fight against Jerusalem and to hinder the progress (Nehemiah 4:8). "Nevertheless we made our prayer unto our God, and set a watch against them day and night, because of them" (Nehemiah 4:9).

The enemy, the devil and the worldly system, is grieved when the church comes with a message that will build lives. They will do everything in their power to hinder the progress. Nevertheless, our cry like Nehemiah's is, "Be not ye afraid of them: remember the Lord, which is great and terrible, and fight for your brethren, your sons, and your daughters, your wives, and your houses" (Nehemiah 4:14).

We must understand that as the church of Jesus Christ seeks to expand the people of the Name, the enemies of truth are not happy. They seek to demoralize, they attempt to label us a cult and make us an object of ridicule. Nehemiah's enemies used these same tactics. They mocked them, asking, "What do these feeble Jews? Will they fortify themselves? Will they sacrifice? Will they make an end in a day? Will they revive the stones out of the heaps of the rubbish which are burned? Now Tobiah the Ammonite was by him, and he said, Even that which they build, if a fox go up, he shall even break down their stone wall" (Nehemiah 4:2-3).

Nehemiah cried, "Hear, O our God; for we are despised: and turn their reproach upon their own head, and give them for a prey in the land of captivity . . . for they have provoked thee to anger before the builders" (Nehemiah 4:4-5).

The result of their prayer and God's help toward them is recorded in Nehemiah 4:6: "So built we the wall; and all the wall was joined together unto the half thereof: for the people had a mind to work." *The people had a MIND TO WORK.*

The battle was not over just because they had a mind to work. The enemy kept conspiring against them to fight and hinder, but they just kept praying (Nehemiah 4:9).

Sanballat hired the Samaritan army to come and threaten war, but the people took up their trowels and continued to build, while everyone had a sword girded by his side. The work went forward even while the enemy kept trying to devise ways to stop it.

The opposition never gives up! They sent unto Nehemiah four times to come down from off the wall. Even Sanballat sent word to Nehemiah to meet together in the plain of Ono to talk things over. Nehemiah's answer was always the same, "I cannot come down, I am doing a good work." The fifth time they sent an open letter to Nehemiah; he went instead to the house of Shemaiah, who was supposed to be on Nehemiah's side, but had been bought off by the enemy. He said to Nehemiah, "Let us meet together in the house of God, within the temple, and let us shut the doors of the temple: for they will come to slay thee; yea, in the night will they come to slay thee" (Nehemiah 6:10).

Nehemiah had the call on him. It was strong in him, so strong that he was not afraid of the enemy. His response to those who were trying to help him was the words of a conqueror: "Should such a man as I flee? and who is there, that, being as I am, would go into the temple to save his life? I will not go in" (Nehemiah 6:11).

Nehemiah knew that God had not sent Shemaiah, but Tobiah and Sanballat had hired him to pronounce this prophecy against him.

Notice Nehemiah's response to this devious plan: "Therefore was he hired, that I should be afraid, and do so, and sin, and that they might have matter for an evil report, that they might reproach me" (Nehemiah 6:13).

Fear is always the tactic the enemy uses to stop God's work. Be careful of those who are *even* in the "temple." If their word does not line up with God's Word, then know that the enemy has hired them to put fear into your heart.

Because Nehemiah chose to listen to God's instructions and not those of someone the enemy had hired, a miracle occurred! Nehemiah 6:15 gives that account: "So the wall was finished in the twenty and fifth day of the month Elul, in fifty and two days." THE MIRACLE WAS THAT THE WALL WAS FINISHED IN FIFTY-TWO DAYS!

Even those who had fought against them and tried to frustrate the purpose had to agree that it was of God. "And it came to pass, that when all our enemies heard thereof, and all the heathen that were about us saw these things, they were much cast down in their own eyes: for they perceived that this work was wrought of our God" (Nehemiah 6:16).

We, too, have been called upon by our God to go into all

17

the world and preach the gospel of Jesus Christ, building churches and establishing works in every continent and city around the globe. It shall be done, for Christ is coming for a GLORIOUS church and it is His will that no one should perish. He will work with us as we endeavor to do this great task that is before us! As the walls were built in fifty-two days, which was miraculous, so shall the end-time results be just as miraculous.

ACKNOWLEDGEMENTS

Thank you, Jack Cunningham, director of Home Missions for the UPCI, for your insight on the subject of unity in chapter three.

Great appreciation is given to J. T. Pugh, former Home Missions director of the UPCI, for the excellent information on the decline of denominations in chapter four.

I give honor to my dear wife, Joy, who took time out of her busy schedule to help put this book together and reach our deadline. I will ever be grateful to her.

"And it came to pass,
when I heard these words,
that I sat down and wept,
and mourned certain days,
and fasted, and prayed
before the God of
heaven."

Nehemiah 1:4

CHAPTER ONE

THE STATE OF THE WORLD

The terrorist attacks on the World Trade Center in New York on September 11, 2001, and the Pentagon in Washington, D.C. forever changed the world. With the crumbling of the towers came great fear and anxiety. The war on terrorists began, but it is a war on an elusive enemy. No one feels quite as safe anymore. The enemy is diabolical and without remorse. They feel as if they are doing these horrible things in the name of their god. Their way of thinking is appalling.

Earthquakes and other natural disasters, as well as

signs in the heavens, are sure indications that the end of days is near. How near? No one knows the day or the hour.

> *"For nation shall rise against nation, and*
> *kingdom against kingdom: and there shall be*
> *famines, and pestilences, and earthquakes,*
> *in divers places."*
> Matthew 24:7

The uncertainties of these times have certainly brought fear and panic to the hearts of this world's population, and our news media brings to us daily the signs of the end times. Mankind has achieved astonishing materialistic progress, but the world is plagued with unhappiness and violence and an ever-increasing moral decay. Scientific and technical knowledge has produced awesome achievements of human knowledge. Yet, over one-third of the world is plagued with the threat of famine. Where millions in one part of the world suffer the quiet devastation of drought and even famine, millions elsewhere are ravaged by violent storms. This planet is in a vicious grip and has a date with destiny.

It is the church's brightest hour, with nation rising against nation and kingdom against kingdom, with economic chaos threatening the world. Many social problems threaten our communities along with the energy crisis. Our world is caught in the clutches of moral decay. With all these frustrations the world faces great dilemma, but these confusions are producing from man an inner feeling for a need of a higher power. This is the reason for the rapid acceleration on the part of mankind throughout the world turning to religion or to God. We know that the higher power is Jesus, and we must tell others about who God really is!

We face throughout the world an avalanche of disease and pestilence. There are incurable diseases, which in spite of medical science, men have been unable to conquer and come up with a cure. Men and women are desperately seeking solutions and medical answers to such diseases as heart failure, AIDS, and cancer that are destroying lives by the tens of thousands and even millions. It is a physically sick world.

RIPE FOR REVIVAL

All of these factors have taken their toll upon the human race. The time is ripe for revival. There must be a group of people in the earth that other people can turn to in this time of crisis. WE ARE THAT PEOPLE. WE HAVE THE TRUTH! WE HAVE THE MESSAGE! WE HAVE THE TOOLS FOR EVANGELISM! WE MUST FALL ON OUR KNEES AND GAIN NEW POWER TO PROCLAIM THE GOSPEL OF JESUS CHRIST, FOR HE IS THE ONLY GOD.

The wave of revival in this decade will be the great revelation of the NAME OF JESUS! THE STAGE HAS BEEN SET. THE STATE OF THE WORLD MAKES IT POSSIBLE FOR GREAT SIGNS AND WONDERS TO BE DONE IN JESUS' NAME!

"And with great power gave the apostles witness
of the resurrection of the Lord Jesus: and great
grace was upon them all."
Acts 4:33

This same power must rest upon us!

POWER OF THE NAME OF JESUS

The early church knew the power of the name of Jesus. When Peter and John went up into the temple to pray, they encountered a lame man who asked for alms. "Then Peter said, Silver and gold have I none; but such as I have give I thee: In the name of Jesus Christ of Nazareth rise up and walk" (Acts 3:6). The church today must have this same revelation of the power of the name of Jesus!

The world is begging for help. It is in their eyes and in the questions that are being asked; we the church have the answers.

Notice the emphasis put on the name of Jesus when Peter and John were asked how the lame man had been able to walk. Peter answered the question by saying, "And his name through faith in his name hath made this man strong, whom ye see and know" (Acts 3:16).

THE PREPARED WILL REAP THE HARVEST

After the bombing of Pearl Harbor by the Japanese and after America dropped the atomic bomb on Hiroshima, the Japanese were devastated and dropped to their knees, greatly humbled. It was at this point that the Americans, led by the late General Douglas MacArthur, took control of the nation of Japan. A short time later, while helping the Japanese people put their lives, economy, world, and nation back together, General MacArthur made an urgent appeal to the United States. He asked all religions, Protestants and Catholics, to please send missionaries to Japan, for they were open for help.

They had trusted in Buddha for so many centuries that they felt like their god would never forsake them and allow them to lose a war. Since this had happened they were groping and searching for something in which they could put their trust. That is why General MacArthur made an appeal to the religious leaders of America to send missionaries. I was made aware of this appeal through my grandparents, Frank and May Gray, who spent a great many years of their lives as missionaries in Japan.

Who was it that sent missionaries to Japan at that time? Few Pentecostal missionaries ever arrived on the shores of Japan. As a matter of fact, there were limited amounts of Protestant missionaries ever to reach Japan. However, the Roman Catholic Church supplied Japan with thousands of missionaries. As a result, who do you suppose reaped the greatest harvest? The people's minds and hearts were open to what the missionaries had to say and as a result of their ripened hearts, the Roman Catholic Church made tremendous inroads into Buddhism.

When the conditions are right the church must move. If we hesitate to thrust forth the sickle and reap the grain, someone else will thrust forth their sickle and reap the ripened grain. Many voices call seductively to modern man, "Follow me, follow me." Unscrupulous cults and false religions claim to give peace and fulfillment that only leads people into bondage and unscriptural practices. Jesus warned about this in Matthew 24. He said that in the latter time many would come in His name declaring themselves to be Christ. He also warned that in the latter time many false prophets would rise and deceive many. When the harvest is ripe, it just depends on who is there to reap. *Whoever is present and prepared is going to reap the harvest.*

Presently, there are many cults who are prepared to reap the harvest. Eastern cults are on the rise according to statistics and are intruding into our universities and colleges of America. Mormon missionaries are in almost every major city in the United States and even in different parts of the world. They are in over 100 nations distributing books of Mormon printed in the language of the nation in which they are being represented. They are being driven with a passion. As a result, their membership is surging higher and higher throughout the world.

The Jehovah Witnesses are infiltrating their doctrine throughout our cities. Every member is considered a minister. They are called Publishers of the Kingdom. Most of them devote an average of fifteen hours a month. Pioneers are required to give at least 100 hours per month. Special pioneers and missionaries devote a minimum of 150 hours per month. They are printing millions of copies of Watchtower literature, Bibles, books, booklets and leaflets that are available in more than 162 languages.

These cults and many others are prepared to reap the harvest. They are not only zealous and enthusiastic in their reaping process, but they are organized in an area of retention and indoctrination. Many people will turn to these cults along with the traditional churches of America and Europe in these troubled times to find security.

While some of these groups have a portion of truth, we must remember that they still do not have all truth. We, the Pentecostals, the Apostolics, with the truth of doctrine, must organize ourselves in this final hour not only to reap the harvest, but also to retain the harvest. IT IS IMPERATIVE TO DO SO!

We must have more FIRE and ZEAL than the cults and

false religions. Truth alone will not save the world, but spreading the gospel will. There will be no rest for the United Pentecostals until the last soul has been reached. We must catch the FIRE of evangelism!

We are not going to evangelize with just methods; we must have the hand of God upon us. We are not going anywhere until there is brokenness. In that brokenness will come God's vision for the church.

"And I said unto the king, If it please the king, and if thy servant have found favour in thy sight, that thou wouldest send me unto Judah, unto the city of my fathers' sepulchres, that I may build it."

Nehemiah 2:5

CHAPTER TWO

THE VISION

The church Jesus founded in Acts 2 was ONE in UNITY, ONE in DOCTRINE, ONE in HOLINESS and ONE in SPIRIT. They were bonded with a common cause to fulfill the great commission. As the years passed into centuries, the enemy destroyed the walls by fragmenting unity, bringing division, introducing false doctrines, and destroying holiness by marriage to the world system. Satan's plan has been to keep the church from becoming one. He is the author of division. He works at causing schism in the body of Christ.

We, the church, even as Nehemiah was called in his day to rebuild the walls, have been called for a specific purpose to rebuild walls.

This is our day! Shakespeare wrote, "There is a tide in the affairs of men which, taken at the flood, leads on to fortune; omitted, all the voyage of their life is bound in shallows and in miseries; we must take the current when it serves or lose our venture" (Julius Caesar, Act IV).

There is a tide, also, in the affairs of God. We will take the current. I BELIEVE ENTIRE CONGREGATIONS WILL BE BAPTIZED IN THE WONDERFUL NAME OF JESUS AND BE FILLED WITH THE SPIRIT!

THE GREAT REVIVAL

The magnitude of the revival that God desires to send in this latter time cannot be accommodated or housed in church buildings or sanctuaries. When Christ referred to the church, He was not referring to the structure, mortar, brick, steel, chandeliers, carpets, stained glass windows, or the towering steeples. He was referring to human beings—the souls of men and women. The whole purpose of His coming into the world was to give Himself as a ransom or sacrifice as stated in John 3:16: "For God so loved the WORLD that he gave his only begotten Son, that whosoever believeth in him should not perish, but have everlasting life."

We do acknowledge the importance of a beautiful building erected for the glory of God and dedicated to the purpose of worship and evangelism. In most cities where a building has been erected, there is a good chance that there will always be a church solidly based in that city.

However, we must acknowledge and face the fact that

the original church in Jerusalem began without its own building. It began in an upper room with 120 being filled with the Spirit. This was the birthday of the church. From there the church grew to 3,000, then to 5,000 and then to multitudes. Soon they were accused of filling Jerusalem with their doctrine. Most historians agree that the church in Jerusalem numbered somewhere between 60,000 to 80,000 of firm believers shortly after the first century.

A building could not be built to house this number of people. It happened so very quickly and rapidly from its birth that it was very important for the church, under the leadership of the Bishop James, to be organized in order to accommodate the rapid growth of harvest that the Lord had sent.

FOLLOWING GOD'S METHODS

One of the greatest sins of our times is that we compare ourselves among ourselves. In so doing we do not do well (II Corinthians 10:12), but we also inhibit the work of God from going forward. Many of us have preconceived ideas and concepts which we have developed through twentieth century methods, when what we should do is revert back to the New Testament church found in the Book of Acts and the Epistles. There we see how God blessed and multiplied those churches with tremendous earthshaking revival.

In many cases we have been quick to follow the methods and patterns of modern day denominational churches, while equally as quick we condemn heresy and false doctrine which they embrace. It is equally important, along with contending for the faith that was once delivered to the saints, and holding to the biblical truth of the Scriptures in theology, that we, likewise, follow the New Testament procedures and methods. This is to assure the rapid growth and the retention that the Lord would have us hold in this mighty revival which God wants to give His church in this latter day.

PREPARATION

In teaching the multitudes, Jesus Christ was very basic and fundamental. He used object lessons and also parables that made it easy for His audience to understand what He was saying. He was never complicated, but simple and practical. Once He discussed the matter of a *sower* that went forth to *sow*. He discussed the *seed* and also the four types of *soil* that were represented in His audience, and concluded this parable by stating:

"Who hath ears to hear, let him hear."
Matthew 13:9

We are all aware that there is a season after the seed has been sown for the rain to fall and the sun to shine, in order for the harvest to be made ripe and ready for gleaning. The tragedy would appear to be that if the harvest were ripe and ready, that the farmer had not taken proper precaution to take the necessary steps to have the harvesters ready for the harvest. If not prepared, the loss would be tragic.

I was raised on a farm in a farming community with ranchers and farmers living all around us. In the fall before the rainy months of winter came, the farmer would break up the ground with a plow or a disc. Then the grain, wheat, barley, or oats would be planted in the fields to be covered by a harrow and left waiting for the heavy rains of winter to fall. During the winter there was very little the farmers could do in the wet fields. They were not idle though. They spent great effort through the winter months preparing the equipment for the time of harvest: over-hauling and oiling the machinery. They were preparing the machinery in such a manner that when the harvest day came, there would be no hesitation. They could not afford to wait until harvest time to prepare the equipment, for they could not lose one day of harvest when the grain was ripe and ready.

Likewise, it is imperative that the church takes every positive step in the direction of preparing for the great harvest that has already started to come. God is sending a mighty ingathering of souls in the end times. If the Apostolic Church is going to benefit from this great end-time harvest, they must be prepared. Comparatively speaking, we must prepare our equipment, our barns and silos, because during harvest time, there is little time to spare, but only to thrust in the sickle.

The story is told in the Gospels of when Christ came to His disciples who had fished all night and had caught nothing, that He spoke a definite command to them: "Cast your nets on the other side." Obeying His voice, even though the night of toil had been fruitless, they were not prepared to hold such a rapid and great ingathering of fish and their net break (Luke 5:6).

There are some that have toiled through the night and had a skimpy harvest, but we cannot allow our nets to weaken. We must prepare with anticipation for the mighty *catch* that the Master would like to give us. May I say, that many precious men of God have labored and toiled and felt that their efforts were unrewarded when they drew their nets in empty or sparsely populated. I would like to urge you to shore up and make strong the nets because when He speaks the harvest will be abundant!

Most of us would agree that we are living just prior to the coming of the Lord and the Lord wants to do a great work in this latter time. He is coming for a glorious church! We must think in terms of entire cities, not with a comfortable feeling. When the church you pastor has reached a growth comparable to another large church, it is unwise to compare yourself with them. The yardstick is not another, but with the *original* church. It is important to think in terms of our entire city, a city that is lost and given over to idolatry. We must think in terms of our nation and our world. Jesus wants us to increase our vision; not only enlarge our vision but to organize our-selves for a great harvest. It is my firm opinion that God will send the harvest according to the preparation of the church.

A BROADER VISION

In many cases, we have limited God and tied His hands by speaking negative thoughts, and talked more about those who have fallen from the faith and the apos-tates of the latter time, than what God will do about the harvest in the end time. Our minds are so cluttered by the environment of our times, that all we can see is the deterioration, judgment, and the annihilation of the human race. If we are not careful, we will miss the whole purpose of the awesome circumstances that exist about us. The current events that have been permitted by God are so that the church can do its great work in this final hour.

We are much like the servant of Elisha, when he was at Dothan. In the early morning hours, the servant stepped to the wall of the little city to take a stroll, but quickly he returned to the lodging place of the prophet in a state of panic, saying to Elisha, "Alas, my master! How shall we do?"

The servant was reacting with fear because he had seen a host of men who surrounded the city with horses and chariots. Fear was a natural response, but there is something bigger than fear. The prophet Elisha could see something in the realm of the Spirit that the servant could not see and responded with these words:

"Fear not: for they that be with us are more than they that be with them."
II Kings 6:16

After he had spoken these words, Elisha told his servant to go take another look. It would be to our advantage to take another look. Sometimes the immediate circumstances have inhibited our faith to what God wishes to do. All we can see and hear is the neighing of the horses, the bustling of the chariots, and the enemies of God and righteousness declaring war against the church; but man's extremities are God's opportunities. When the servant took the second look, the Lord opened his eyes to see the innumerable angelic host. Then the servant understood what the prophet meant when he said, "There are more with us than with them."

There is the story in Mark 5 of Jairus, the ruler of the synagogue, who sought Jesus out to heal his sick daughter who was nigh unto death. On the way to the house before Christ arrived, a messenger came and told the ruler that it was not necessary to bother Jesus, for the daughter had already died. When Jesus heard what the servant spoke to the ruler, He said these words:

"Be not afraid, only believe."
Mark 5:36

Before they had even reached the doorstep of the home, they heard the wailing and the crying which told them that the daughter was dead. But when Jesus stepped into the home, He said, "The damsel is not dead, but sleepeth." They laughed Him to scorn. They did not look upon Him as Jesus Christ, the Son of God, or as the resurrection and the life, or as One who had the power to speak life back into the deceased body. To them, He was just another religious leader.

If we are not careful, we will begin to feel that we are just another church group, just another denomination. We are more than that! We are the church, the New Testament church, the church of the living God. What we must do is what Jesus did. He sent them all out of the room, every negative thinker and unbeliever. He then took into the room Peter, James, John, and the mother and father, and closed the door on all unbelief. Then He spoke life back into the deceased girl's body.

We hear sounds and voices from all over indicating that it cannot be done: that we cannot build great churches, cannot win our cities, cannot lead men and women to Jesus Christ because the way is too straight and narrow and that nobody wants this Pentecostal way.

It is time to cast those thoughts and voices outside the door. Close the door on them and determine not to listen to one negative thought. We must rebuke the spirit of unbelief and accept the promises of God. Preach faith and teach faith and God will send a mighty revival.

It is the will of God to send great revival through the medium of His church. The church is where the revival must start, if the world is to be touched. The VISION must be greater than the negative voices around us.

> "Where there is no vision, the people perish."
>
> Proverbs 29:18

THE PASTOR

Let us come to a clear focus on this matter. If the church is the key to revival, then the pastor is the key to the church. There seems little hope of reviving some congregations unless the minister can first be revived. The pastor can block it or bless it. He is a man under authority and with authority. The Bible speaks about him being a star in the right hand of Jesus (Revelation 1:20).

Stars are symbols of rule and authority shown in Genesis 1:18. The pastor has tremendous authority whether he is *for* something or *against* something. He is the most powerful man in the congregation. He has more power than any evangelist who may come and go. He can make or break a congregation. That is why God takes time to develop and mold the pastor. The churches are the golden *lampstands* in the cities and the ministers are the means of *lighting* them.

The seven letters in Revelation, chapters two and three, are letters to the churches. Most of them are revival messages to the congregations, and when God wants to talk to the church, He talks to the minister, the *angel* of the church. In each case, if the pastor gets the message, the church will get it also.

Here is a tremendous truth. Here is God's very revelation on the subject of church revival. Like priest; like people. The congregation seldom rises above the level of the pastor. Water reaches its own level.

> **Every pastor must first catch the vision, then ask God for an anointing to reach his congregation and infuse within them a fire of passion to reach every soul by whatever method they can use to impart this truth!**

What we need today is a growing ministry if we are to have growing churches. If the ministry is revived, the church will be revived. If the pastor is a man of faith, the church will be a church of faith. Faith is expressed by our acts. We will receive from God according to our faith. If a farmer expects to reap a great harvest, he will prepare accordingly.

ATTEMPT GREAT THINGS

Years ago someone gave me a plaque with a statement by William Carey which said, "Attempt great things for God, expect great things from God."

Those words had a profound effect upon my ministry,

for I believe that if we attempt great things for the Lord, then in return we can expect mighty things at the hand of God.

The first century church attempted great and mighty things for God. As a result they likewise expected great acts from the Lord. The Thessalonican Jews, after observing the mighty work of the Early Church, cried to the rulers of the city,

> *"These that have turned the world upside down are come hither also."*
> Acts 17:6

It all started with Paul, who had entered the city and preached and reasoned with the Jews in the synagogue. After several weeks some believed and became followers, as did a great number of devout priests. That is when the leaders of the Jewish community forcibly brought certain Christians before the city authorities and made their protest.

The early Christians *believed* they could change the world. There was not a question in their minds that the world could be changed, if they were willing to pay the price. They did not permit negative thoughts to enter their minds. They believed every city, every village, every country they entered into, would be affected by the gospel. Night and day

> **The early church believed they could do it!**

they lived with confidence that the world would be turned upside down through the Apostolic Ministry.

ONE WORLD

There has been much talk about a one-world government, but there will never be a total one-world government until the one eternal God, Jesus Christ, sits on the throne during the millenium and reigns for 1,000 years. Nevertheless, God died for ONE WORLD, and that is every culture, every nationality: all people.

America has become the great Babylon of the latter days. This is the nation of every nationality. They have migrated from every nation. Some have referred to it as *The Modern Day Babylon.*

We, as ministers of the gospel, pastors, and people of local congregations, must change our concepts and conceive that this is a God-given opportunity—to reach every nationality in America.

The Books of Joel and Acts both refer to the prophecy, "that in the last days God's Spirit would be poured out upon all flesh," which means all nationalities. The church will never succeed in reaching America unless we realize the opportunity that is set before us. In some cases the receptivity of many of these different cultures far exceeds the receptivity of the Anglo Saxons toward the gift of the Holy Spirit.

I commend the Home Missions Division for the multicultural thrust of evangelism, but it must reach every city.

DAUGHTER WORKS

In the last decade there has been a great thrust for pastors to establish daughter works, satellite works, extensions, etc., in the UPCI in America. Many of these are multi-cultural works. This is absolutely God's fulfillment of the vision for our day. At this point I urge earnestly that pastors all across this fellowship enlarge their vision to incorporate daughter works and preaching points.

It is not God's will for us to win people to this experience and then send them out to the wolves to be devoured. When they are caught in the net, we must bring them into the boat. When the harvest is ripe, we must not let it spoil in the field. Where the flock of sheep have grown, it is important not to let them scatter over the fields to be devoured by wild beasts, but we must know them by name in order to give an account of them and to make sure they are all in the fold. That is why it is necessary to have small group ministries.

OUR VISION: I have spoken to Jack Cunningham, the Home Missions director, and we have agreed that our vision should be the following: If in the year 2002 we can get 1,000 churches in the United States and Canada combined to establish one daughter work, we will have gained 1,000 new churches. This is altogether possible, and would be very pleasing to God. Churches and pastors that will apply this principle of multiplication will find that in doing so the law of the harvest works. The local assembly will never lose, for the God of the harvest blesses the church that continually gives.

SMALL GROUP MINISTRIES

The most progressive and largest churches in America and in the world are involved in small group ministries. This concept was first conceived in the Book of Acts: "And they continuing daily with one accord in the temple, and breaking bread from house to house, did eat their meat with gladness and singleness of heart" (Acts 2:46).

Paul refers to the church that was in the house of Priscilla and Aquilla in Romans 16: "Likewise greet the church that is in their house" (Romans 16:5). As you grow your congregation will be blessed by incorporating into its organization small group ministries.

> # The church must speak the same things!

As pastors, we have many capable people that can share in our ministry. We have many talented people that we pastor, who could help in this ministry. They can never take the place of a pastor, but they can assist him. These groups are always under pastoral authority. One of the sure ways for this to happen is to have good communication and weekly meetings. The church can never survive without unity. They must speak the same things.

There are many people who will not visit a church because it represents an establishment, but they will come to a home. Of course, they will eventually come to the church as truth finds its way into their hearts.

We must organize our churches and our laymen into groups and teach them leadership responsibilities of shepherding in order to hold the ingathering and the great revival that will produce thousands upon tens of thousands of brand new babes in Christ. This is not to replace corporate worship, but to augment it. If we have trained shepherds, men and women who love the souls of the newborns, we will be in a position to accommodate this great latter time harvest.

GOD'S REQUIREMENT

God is asking more of the end-time church than any preceding generation. "To whom much is given, much is required." We have been given more than those who have gone before us. We have more resources, finances, talents, technology, and opportunities.

We must look toward God, cleanse ourselves, and go forward in Jesus' name to reach a world. In Isaiah 6, the account is given of Isaiah's vision. First, he saw the Lord: it was an *upward* vision. Secondly, he saw himself: it was an *inward* vision. Thirdly, he saw the world: an *outward* vision. As we, like Isaiah, look upward we will see the Lord in all His holiness; as we look inward, we will see ourselves and our need for cleansing; and as we look outward we will see a world that is in need of a Savior.

> God is asking more of the end-time church than any preceding generation. **"To whom much is given, much is required."**

"Then said I unto them,
Ye see the distress that we
are in, how Jerusalem lieth
waste, and the gates thereof
are burned with fire; come,
and LET US BUILD up the
wall of Jerusalem, that we
be no more a reproach."

Nehemiah 2:17

CHAPTER THREE

THE CHURCH

It is the hour for a new wave, a wave of the Holy Spirit and revelation of the name of our God and baptism in that name: JESUS! United Pentecostal Church International, it *is* our hour! This is the day that was spoken of by the prophet Joel:

> *"And it shall come to pass in the last days, saith God, I will pour out of my Spirit upon all flesh: and your sons and your daughters shall prophesy, and your young men shall see*

*visions, and your old men shall dream
dreams: And on my servants and on my
handmaidens I will pour out in those days of
my Spirit; and they shall prophesy."*
Acts 2:17-18

The grass roots of this organization are very critical to growth. We are all members of the body and there should be no condescending attitudes or "big folks and little folks." Naturally there are those among us that are greatly respected for their anointing and giftedness and the great contribution they have made to the kingdom of God, but if they are truly of God, they will be humble and kind with no arrogance.

This is an organization of preachers. Thus, as a God-called man or woman you are an integral part. Everyone is important for the evangelization of the world. A chain is only as strong as its weakest link. We will strengthen the weak areas among us and prepare to reach the world.

PURPOSE OF ORGANIZATION

The purpose of the UPCI is to bring together men and women of like precious faith. Number one, in so doing we strengthen one another in having common objectives and purpose. Number two is the joining of hands and resources for the sole purpose of evangelization of the world. For we know that everyone outside of the gospel of Jesus Christ is lost. The right to exist as the UPCI must always be predicated upon these two important and imperative facts. All other reasons are by products, as good as they are. The benefits of organization are many. Two can do more than one if properly organized. "Two are better than one; because they have a good reward for their labour. For if they fall, the one will lift up his fellow; but woe to him that is alone when he falleth; for he hath not another to help him up. Again, if two lie together, then they have heat: but how can one be warm alone? And if one prevail against him, two shall withstand him; and a threefold cord is not quickly broken" (Ecclesiastes 4:9-12).

"How should one chase a thousand, and two put ten thousand to flight."
Deuteronomy 32:30

THE PROCESS OF ORGANIZATION

We must all agree that when we make decisions by the body that we live by those decisions. We do not always get our way, but we respect that which is decided by the body. If we feel the decision is wrong, we do not manifest a rebellious spirit; we simply work to change it.

The UPCI is a fast growing movement. The people who are a part of it are the "salt of the earth." Churches are springing up everywhere. Just as Sanballat and Tobiah attempted to discredit the work of Nehemiah and brand it a failure, so are those who would do the same about us today.

PEOPLE SKILLS

Love is more than a word. It is Jesus reaching in love toward others through us. Every revival will be where there is great love manifested toward one another. Love is always where miracles are found.

Troublemakers: There will always be troublemakers in the church, but the pulpit should never become the battleground. The whole body should not be demoralized because of one or two problems. The FIRE of the Holy Ghost and godly wisdom will help burn out those problems.

People skills are wrapped up in being courteous and kind to all those you come in contact with, and treating others as you would like to be treated. It is just plain, honest to goodness kindness, not expecting anything in return.

"He that loveth not knoweth not God; for God is love" (I John 4:8).

FINANCES

It is never the will of God for the apparent lack of finances to hinder or throttle our evangelistic thrust. God is our provider! As we step through the doors of opportunity, God will provide through His people sufficient funds to evangelize this world whether it be foreign missions, home missions, or our own local cities and communities.

Stepping out by faith by pastors and churches is essential!

Perhaps many of us need to take a look at our own lifestyle. As pastors we are in a unique situation. Many of us control the finances of our own local assemblies, and I know that most of you find yourselves stretching for more in order to accommodate your local vision.

May I suggest, "Let's take another look at the total picture." Maybe God is asking us to be more frugal. Let us make sure our priorities of commitment are to reach the lost.

Faith giving is very important, as well as the element of sacrifice.

If we want God to supply our needs, we must supply His kingdom with sufficient funds to reach the world. This is declared in the story of the Philippian Church.

"Now ye Philippians know also, that in the beginning of the gospel, when I departed from Macedonia, no church communicated with me as concerning giving and receiving, but ye only."
Philippians 4:15

Because of their commitment to missions, Paul gave them this promise, which is still true for the church today:

"But my God shall supply all your need according to his riches in glory by Christ Jesus."
Philippians 4:19

CHILDREN'S MINISTRY

It is important to have a strong children's ministry, even if there are only a few children. We cannot afford to lose our children to the devil and the world. The Sunday School Division has provided material for children's ministry, and now there are conferences held for the leaders of this very important ministry. Along with the other functions of our local assemblies in 2002 there must be a great focus on child evangelism and revival amongst the children and indoctrination of the Word. We must win them while they are young! Tens of thousands of children are awaiting the gospel. What a truly ripe field!

YOUTH MINISTRY

OUR VISION: The United Pentecostal Church has the most dedicated and committed young people in the world. Their zeal will be channeled; they will be given an opportunity to serve their God as young people serve their country. We should not allow the Jehovah Witnesses, the Mormons, and the Muslims to be more organized amongst their young than we are. There is no doubt in my mind that if we develop the proper plan and proper supervision that we have hundreds of young people that would give a year or two years of their life to this latter-day harvest. Their lives would be enriched going all over the world teaching Bible studies and fulfilling the commission Jesus gave: "Go ye into all the world, and preach the gospel to every creature" (Mark 16:15).

Jesus will be with them as He was with the early church: "And they went forth, and preached every where, the Lord working with them, and confirming the word with signs following" (Mark 16:20).

MISSIONS

Missionaries are called, but how can they go unless they are sent? Collectively, we as pastors must keep before our churches the great need for missions.

OUR VISION: The vision of world evangelism must be conceived in the minds of the United Pentecostals globally. Not only must missionaries be sent from North America, but they must also be sent from some of the more powerful and established works in other countries. Together with a coordinated effort we can send forth more than 100 missionaries a year. This too is the vision of the latter times.

Whether small or large, every church must put forth the effort to have a Faith Promise service.

FOREIGN MISSIONS

There are presently 237 career missionaries and 97 intermediate missionaries. The third level of missionary service known as *associates in missions* now has 177. This gives us a total of 511 missionaries. There are in overseas fields 20,666 national ministers preaching this glorious gospel in 142 nations.

> We are the church! There is one world Jesus died for. There is one message. Our vision is to reach them.

During the 2000 calendar year, a total of 124,896 were baptized in Jesus' name and 123,030 received the baptism of the Holy Ghost. Over 337 received the Holy Ghost every day of the year, and over 342 were baptized in Jesus' name each day of the year.

In talking with Brother Harry Scism, our retiring Foreign Missions director, he informed me that we have well over three million constituents in foreign lands. As of October 2001 we now have in foreign countries 28,416 congregations.

HOME MISSIONS

Every week there are services conducted in 52 different languages in North America. In 2001 there were 423 daughter works, 367 preaching points, and 469 home missionary status churches making a total of 1,259 new home mission works. We are very thankful for this rapid growth. Adding all this together with the existing churches we are getting very close to 5,000 congregations in North America.

THE PUBLISHED WORD

Acts 13:49 says, "And the word of the Lord was published throughout all the region."

The power of the printed Word can never be underestimated. The United Pentecostal Church is blessed with an exceptionally well-managed Publishing House which includes a computer design and printing department. Word Aflame, the Editorial Division, provides incredible material (which every congregation should take advantage of).

Our generation is a reading generation. Let's give them the best! Publish it in an attractive way that the world will devour it. The Word will not return void.

I recently spoke with our newly elected Foreign Mission director, Bruce Howell, as we discussed publishing the Word in connection with evangelizing the world. It occurred to us that we could set up small printing plants all around the world, thus printing in many languages, which would enable us to reach multitudes. This is altogether possible. Perhaps even buying some model 360 AB Dick presses so that people can operate them even with limited training.

GUARD AGAINST DECLINE

There is a vast exodus in the old mainline denominations in America. Many evangelicals and so-called Pentecostals are on the decline. When a movement ceases to emphasize heart transformation and the infilling of the Holy Ghost it loses its momentum, for without the Spirit of God there is no power!

The following information gives seven reasons why denominations decline:

1. *Denial*: rationalizing; refusing to see reality of losses.
2. *Liberalism*: Do not ever discount the energy and commitment of "True Believers."
3. *Inflated Tolerance*: No such thing as absolute truth. Tolerance is a virtue but inflated tolerance dilutes truth and weakens churches.
4. *Misplaced Priorities*: Evangelism must be primary not simply improvement of society; not existing to be service organizations.
5. *Becoming Adverse to Evangelism*: We will not try to convert anyone unless we believe they need to be converted.
6. *Distrust of Spiritual Leadership*
7. *Suspicion*

"And I said unto the king, If it please the king, and if thy servant have found favour in thy sight, that **thou wouldest send me . . .**"

Nehemiah 2:5

CHAPTER FOUR

OUR MISSION

There are five things needed to fulfil our mission:

- TRUTH
- SPIRIT
- UNITY
- ZEAL
- VISION

The United Pentecostal Church International is a church of destiny! We are a movement that has been commissioned for this FINAL HOUR. We have the biblical truth that the New Testament church taught and that

Jesus set forth in His instructions to His disciples. We have His Spirit within us, although we need to be baptized anew with a fresh touch of His Spirit. We need to be more unified in our approach in reaching the world. We are not an island unto ourselves, but we are integrally woven together by the blood of Jesus Christ. We cannot allow ourselves to be laid back or filled with apathy. There is need for more zeal and passion among us. This book will give a clear sound of what our vision is. The time is ripe; we must move into the field for it is ripe unto harvest.

"Therefore said he [Jesus] unto them,
The harvest truly is great, but the labourers
are few: pray ye therefore the Lord of the
harvest, that he would send forth
labourers into his harvest."
Luke 10:2

SENT

As Nehemiah was sent by King Artaxerxes, so our King has also sent us on a mission. It is our greatest mission in life. King Jesus is our example. He gave His life for the people of this world. It was His mission.

"Pilate therefore said unto him, Art thou a
king then? Jesus answered, Thou sayest that I
am a king. To this end was I born, and for
this cause came I into the world, that I should
bear witness unto the truth. Every one that is
of the truth heareth my voice."
John 18:37

In Luke 10:1, Jesus sent seventy disciples out into the harvest field two by two. Jesus sends His disciples forth as shown in John 20:21: "Then said Jesus to them again, Peace be unto you: as my Father hath sent me, even so send I you."

We can never forget who has sent us into this world to preach the gospel. It should be pulsating through our veins, throbbing in our minds, "I am sent on a mission. I am sent on a mission by God Almighty to do His bidding." Every day should be looked upon as an adventure into a world characterized by His Spirit.

As Nehemiah was released by the king to do what God had put in his heart to do, we the church have been released. As he was equipped for the job, the Spirit has equipped us. As Nehemiah considered the need and state of affairs and told the people that the hand of God was upon him, so must the church do the same!

THE COMMISSION

The United Pentecostal Church International is right at four million constituents, and we have 33,500+ congregations worldwide. Sounds significant, but it is like Gideon in comparison to the world. We have been commissioned to go into the whole world and preach the gospel. "Go ye into all the world, and preach the gospel to every creature" (Mark 16:15).

WE CAN MAKE A DIFFERENCE!

The power to witness and do all the things Jesus intended for the church to do as the anointed ones would bring about the fulfillment of the Great Commission and thus it would be said about us, "These that have turned the world upside down are come hither also" (Acts 17:6).

PASSION

"Unction cannot be learned, only earned—by prayer." The two prerequisites to success in God are vision and passion, both of which are born in and maintained by prayer.

We are commanded to be, "Fervent in spirit, serving the Lord" (Romans 12:11).

Galatians 4:18, "It is good to be zealously affected always in a good thing."

Now, more than ever before, the church must be zealously passionate about spreading the good news of the gospel of Jesus Christ.

Nothing could throttle the passion of the early church. It penetrated into Caesar's household. The FIRE and PASSION broke through the pagan walls of darkness and brought light into the Gentile world. Though the resistance of the heathen produced grave persecution, nothing could hinder the Pentecostal experience and message from spreading into every region, country, and continent of the world.

Even today the church is passionately declaring the gospel in nations around the world at the expense of persecution. Passionate believers are proclaiming Christ in Russia, China, Saudi Arabia, and other countries that have had "underground" churches for many years.

Passion does not stop at anything. It is a floodtide of power that will sweep aside any obstacle that hell puts in its way.

When the rushing mighty wind of the Spirit, the

breath of God, blew through the upper room and cloven tongues like as of FIRE, sat upon each one, spontaneous combustion took place that ignited into a worldwide revival. The FIRE of the Spirit became uncontrollable, unpredictable, and irresistible to those who felt its power. The Sanhedrin could not control this FIRE, nor could they predict where the FIRE would break out next. It was a raging, massive FIRE that could not be quenched by persecution, false accusations, or even death!

This is the kind of passionate FIRE that is needed by the whole church today. When this becomes a reality, there will be unprecedented revival FIRES that will burn all around the world.

UNITY

In order for the mission to be accomplished, the people must willingly cry, "Let us rise up and build." Nehemiah 2:18: "Then I told them of the hand of my God which was good upon me; as also the king's words that he had spoken unto me. And they said, Let us rise up and build. So they strengthened their hands for this good work." They worked together for one common cause.

Ephesians 4:1-6 states: "I therefore, the prisoner of the Lord, beseech you that ye walk worthy of the vocation wherewith ye are called. With all lowliness and meekness, with longsuffering, forbearing one another in love; Endeavoring to KEEP THE UNITY of the Spirit in the bond of peace. There is ONE BODY, and ONE SPIRIT, even as ye are called in ONE HOPE of your calling; ONE LORD, ONE FAITH, ONE BAPTISM, ONE GOD and Father of all, who is above all, and through all, and in you all."

Endeavoring means to make a concerted effort toward; an earnest attempt; to (give) diligence to and to labor after. Sometimes it is work to keep the UNITY, but it is worth it. In the preceding verse, Paul tells how to *keep the unity.* The task is accomplished by *forbearing one another. Forbearing* means to put up with one another; bear with one another, and to endure one another.

It is ONE all the way through to the end. We are ONE in Christ. Benjamin Franklin once said, "On the matter before us, if we do not hang together, gentlemen, we will most assuredly hang separately." With equal vigor and determination, the United Pentecostal Church International must *hang together* or the enemy will separate us so that he can destroy us.

The following story is taken from my book *Baptism of Fire,* which proves the power of unity:

> *Aesop tells us that there were four bulls which were good friends. They went every where together, fed together, and lay down to rest together, always keeping so close to each other that if any danger were near they could all face it at once.*
>
> *Now there was a lion which had determined to have them, but he could never get at them singly. He was a match for any one alone, but not for all four at once. However, he used to watch for his opportunity, and, when one lagged the least bit behind the others as they grazed, he would slink up and whisper that the other bulls had been saying unkind things about him. This he did so often that at last the four friends became uneasy. Each thought the other three were plotting against him.*

Finally, as there was no trust among them, they went off by themselves, their friendship broken.

This was what the lion wanted. One by one he killed them, and made four good meals.

Likewise, this is the devil's strategy. As in the story of Nehemiah, the enemy tried to scare them and fragment them, confusing their minds, but Nehemiah told them, "Stay working together on the wall; don't leave because of the taunts of the enemy. Just keep doing what the Lord has told us to do."

The church started with a group of people being in ONE PLACE, in ONE ACCORD, praying and waiting for ONE THING: the gift of the Holy Spirit.

At the UPCI World Conference in Athens, Greece, leaders from every nation were asked to speak ten minutes. One after another they spoke on UNITY. One of the brethren said, *"We don't pray for revival, we pray for unity."* Revival will come when we are united. Divisions, schisms, envy, and strife are the enemies of revival.

Jesus prayed a prayer in John 17:21 that is still echoing down through the ages: "That they all may be ONE; as thou, Father, art in me, and I in thee, that they also may be ONE in us."

People often affix importance to a biblical subject based on how many times it is mentioned in the Scriptures.

The following list are important subjects and how many times they are mentioned in the Bible:

- Tithes   25
- Holy Ghost   90
- Water Baptism   100

- Fasting 102
- Prayer 114
- Offerings 265
- Gathered Together 97
- Together 484

Nothing can restrain a people who are ONE in spirit, ONE in purpose, and who are in ONE mind! This is proven in the story told in Genesis 11:5-6:

> *"And the LORD came down to see the city and the tower, which the children of men builded. And the LORD said, Behold, the people is one, and they have all one language; and this they begin to do: and now nothing will be restrained from them, which they have imagined to do."*

God said that nothing could restrain a people from accomplishing their goal as long as they spoke the same things, worked together for the same goals, and were ONE in spirit. This is what God wants for the United Pentecostal Church International: There is ONE GOD, ONE WORLD, ONE CHURCH, and ONE VISION.

THE TASK

The task at times seems difficult, but we must remember we are not doing it in our own power as so powerfully stated in Zechariah 4:6: "Then he answered and spake unto me, saying, This is the word of the LORD unto Zerubbabel, saying, Not by might, nor by power, but by my spirit, saith the LORD of hosts."

Gideon had only 300 men to fight against the great host of the Midianites, but by following God's instructions and by His Spirit, they won the war.

Jesus chose twelve men as His disciples and from this small beginning, Christianity has grown in great proportions. It was a group of 120 men and women in an upper room in Jerusalem that first received the outpouring of His Spirit and who were baptized in His name. It started small, but it did not remain small. In the space of two years all of Asia had heard the gospel of Jesus Christ. "And this continued by the space of two years; so that all they which dwelt in Asia heard the word of the Lord Jesus, both Jews and Greeks" (Acts 19:10).

> "Not by might, nor by power, but by my spirit saith the LORD!"

NUMBERS

Someone might say, "I'm not as big as this guy over here, I can't do anything." You may have a church of thirty-five, but it should not remain at that figure. If it is God's church it is going to grow. Anything that is alive will grow.

Some people have a mentality of smallness. We once had a couple in our church that said they were going to leave our church because it was getting too big. I told them, "That's fine, but you are going to go into a little church because it is comfortable to you, but if it is God's church it is going to grow."

CAPACITY: As John and Charles Wesley were once praying, Charles, who was receiving a great blessing, said, "My God, I can't stand anymore. You're so great!" John, his brother, corrected him by saying, "Don't tell God you can't stand it anymore. Ask him to increase your capacity."

This is what needs to happen among us. Jesus talks about people bringing forth fruit, "some thirtyfold, some sixty, and some an hundred" (Matthew 13:8, 23; Mark 4:8, 20).

If you are at a thirtyfold capacity, ask God to increase you to sixty. If you are at sixty, ask God to increase you to eighty. If you are at a hundred, ask Him to double that. We need to be increasing ourselves. Pray, "God, enable me to increase my vision." If you have a vision then you will have a burden to achieve it.

NO RETIREMENT

Romans 11:29 states, "For the gifts and calling of God are without repentance." There is no retirement. When God calls a man, he is called forever.

A called man of God after many years may change from carrying the heavy load of administration to more teaching, travelling, and helping others, but if he is called there is no stopping.

We must go to the time of departure as Paul said, "For I am now ready to be offered, and the time of my departure is at hand. I have fought a good fight, I have finished my course, I have kept the faith. Henceforth there is laid up for me a crown of righteousness, which the Lord, the righteous judge, shall give me at that day: and not to me only, but unto all them also that love his appearing" (II Timothy 4:6-8).

Every called minister must work until the Lord comes

or until he is called home, but in a different way as he grows older.

DISTRACTIONS

1. *Our Foe*: Satan. Ephesians 6:12 states: "For we wrestle not against flesh and blood, but against principalities, against powers, against the rulers of the darkness of this world, against spiritual wickedness in high places."

   He wants to hinder revival! That is his business.

   Several years ago in the city where I was pastor, there occurred a tragic event at one of the local schools. A young man created a distraction while the children were playing on the playground. He set a car on fire in front of the school. While the teachers responsible for watching the children were focusing on the burning car, the demented man murdered five of the children while they were at play.

   Satan has created many distractions in order to divert the attention of the church and the pastor away from their true purpose. He creates church trouble or problems and more problems. He will do anything to keep us from focusing on the ONE thing Jesus called us to do: Reach the lost!

   The devil would have us believe the church is to be a social club. While it is important for the church to have its social times, and the man of God to have his recreation time, there must be a balance.

2. *Focusing on the wrong things*. It is imperative to have a right spirit, stay focused on our mission, keep the vision clear, and to preach the Word.

I Corinthians 10:6 names five things which caused the children of Israel to wander in the wilderness instead of reaching their promised land: "Now these things were our examples, to the intent we should not lust after evil things, as they also lusted."

a. Lust
b. Idolatry
c. Fornication
d. Tempting Christ
e. Murmuring

3. *Fear*. When Shemaiah came to Nehemiah it was first with anger and ridicule. They tried every conceivable way to stop the building up of the walls, but they saved FEAR for their last tactic. Nehemiah recognized what they were trying to do and immediately called it by what it was—an evil report. Notice also Nehemiah said that if he would have listened to their report and been afraid that he would have sinned. "Therefore was he hired, that I should be afraid, and do so, and sin, and that they might have matter for an evil report, that they might reproach me" (Nehemiah 6:13). The enemy's tactics are so that God's children can be reproached for their fear and lack of trusting in the Lord. We must go forward no matter how many Shemaiah's speak their words of fear and doubt!

NEVER GIVE UP!

Set your face as a flint. The enemy sent opposition five different times to Nehemiah, but he always had the same answer, "We are doing a great work, and we can't come down." Just as the enemy never wants to give up, so should the church be just as relentless, never giving up until the task is completed.

"For the builders, every one had his sword girded by his side, and so builded. And he that sounded the trumpet was by me."

Nehemiah 4:18

CHAPTER FIVE

OUR MESSAGE

It is time to sound the trumpet loud and clear as never before. The work must go forward with the sword kept close to us. The sword is the Word of God. Ephesians 6:17 declares: "And take the helmet of salvation, and the sword of the Spirit, which is the word of God."

IS THERE A DIFFERENCE?

Our message is a very positive message. There are no ifs and ands; it is absolutely predicated upon the Holy

Scripture. The Scripture is so profoundly clear and sure that there is little room for error.

There is a difference! Many religious groups in Christianity take their message from the traditional church, which has been drastically altered through the years from generation to generation, perhaps before, but especially beginning with the Council of Nicea 325 A.D. From this time there was a radical change from the original New Testament church. Thus, what we teach and believe and preach is vastly different from traditional teaching of Christianity. Our message must always be predicated upon Scripture, never tradition. The Holy Scripture is our blueprint. The Book of Acts is our pattern. This message, if preached and obeyed, saves from sin, keeps one from sin, and delivers one from bondage. It is a supernatural message and produces miraculous results. It is a message the world needs. It is never to be watered down.

Living in a world that is infested with drugs, alcohol, and sexual perversion with demented and twisted minds, this message that we preach brings emancipation from those chains. Thus, our message is more than a social gospel; it is a gospel of deliverance from bondage.

Our churches, as a result of biblical preaching, should thrive with old-time Apostolic power and revival.

Just think, we have the most powerful gospel in all the world! Every morning when we wake up, we ought to thank God for this precious truth and for the wonderful Word of God which is so fresh and true.

As ministers of the gospel, we should earnestly seek God's anointing upon our ministry so that we can deliver this sacred truth with unction. Every United Pentecostal Church, daughter work, and preaching point must become a hot spot of revival where the truth is boldly declared! Thus, let it be known and noised abroad that we have become revival centers boldly proclaiming the message of the Scripture.

It must be proclaimed without compromise that there is ONE GOD according to the Scripture: the ONLY GOD and that HIS NAME IS JESUS, and without Him there is no salvation, for He is the DOOR to eternal life! This ONE GOD manifested Himself as Father in creation, and Son in redemption, and the Holy Spirit in regeneration and empowerment.

Paul declared in Romans 1:16: "For I am not ashamed of the gospel of Christ: for it is the power of God unto salvation to every one that believeth; to the Jew first, and also to the Greek." IT IS THE POWER!

There are other religions that believe in one God: the Muslims and Jews. We, the United Pentecostal Church International, are a group of believers who have experienced Pentecost, and who follow the apostles and prophets of Jesus Christ, the chief cornerstone. There are many religious groups who believe in one God, but they do not proclaim the name of Jesus as that ONE GOD.

Degenerate men must be born again according to John 3:5. Peter gave the formula for this new birth experience in Acts 2:38: "Then Peter said unto them, Repent, and be baptized every one of you in the name of Jesus Christ for the remission of sins, and ye shall receive the gift of the Holy Ghost."

If we preach this profound truth with FIRE, LOVE, and ANOINTING, we will witness the awesome results.

1. *There is a difference in our message of salvation!* We are a people of the name of Jesus! Jesus

did not say that we would be hated because we speak in tongues or do miracles, but He said we would be hated because of His name. This is stated in Matthew 10:22: "And ye shall be hated of all men for my name's sake: but he that endureth to the end shall be saved." (See also Mark 13:13; Luke 21:17.)

2. *There is a difference in our message of holiness!* "But ye are a chosen generation, a royal priesthood, an holy nation, a peculiar people; that ye should shew forth the praises of him who hath called you out of darkness into his marvelous light" (I Peter 2:9).

Holiness is very important to God. There is biblical holiness that is different from worldly standards. The difference is not just holiness; the difference is we are set apart. We are the anointed ones baptized in His name and with Holy Ghost fire.

Sin must be dealt with. There are times when we deal with issues of holiness, but first holiness is a state of the heart. You can line up the outside, but sometimes people remain with "dead men's bones" on the inside of their heart.

To be holy means to be separated from sin and consecrated to God and His ideas. It is being separated from the world system and being in harmony with God. The reason for God's demand for men and women to be holy is that He wants them to be like Him. "Ye shall be holy: for I the LORD your God am holy" (Leviticus 19:2).

II Corinthians 7:1 commands us to cleanse ourselves and aim at perfect holiness: "Having therefore these promises, dearly beloved, let us cleanse ourselves from all filthiness of the flesh and spirit, perfecting holiness in the fear of God."

God has called His church to holiness: "For God hath not called us unto uncleanness, but unto holiness" (I Thessalonians 4:7).

II Corinthians 6:17 commands, "Wherefore come out from among them, and be ye separate, saith the Lord, and touch not the unclean thing; and I will receive you."

Christians should avoid all appearance of evil instead of doing a balancing act on the line of demarcation between good and evil: "Abstain from all appearance of evil" (I Thessalonians 5:22).

If the heart is right, you have a good foundation to teach the outer standards: HAIR, MODEST APPAREL and SHAMEFACEDNESS and HOLY LIVING.

There is a right way to deal with it. What Hollywood has produced on television by its evils is destroying families, teenagers, and the souls of many. Television perpetuates evil and is a thief of time, helping to destroy the mission of the church.

Holiness is a spirit, and begins on the inside of a person. The cleanliness of Christ must begin in the heart. However, true holiness will certainly spread throughout the body, mind, and spirit, thus affecting the outer person, their talk, actions and dress.

The glory of God must rest upon every born again believer so that people would look upon them and say, "I want what they have!" This is portrayed in the holiness of our spirit, attitude, dress, and demeanor.

Let the world say as the Greeks said to Philip, "Sir, we would see Jesus" (John 12:21). LET US SHOW THE WORLD JESUS!

"And the king granted me,
according to the good hand
of my God upon me."

Nehemiah 2:8

CHAPTER SIX

OUR HOUR

God's hand is upon the church. He is granting His people with favor from on high. He is opening doors that could not open without Him. Many opportunities to witness to other denominations, congregations, and ministers in America have occurred, while in other countries entire groups of churches are receiving this blessed truth, and this is being brought about by the great will of our God.

As Nehemiah found favor with his earthly king, we have found favor with our heavenly King. He is sending us forth as a mighty army to share with the millions of people who have not received this glorious gospel of Jesus Christ.

THIS IS OUR DAY!

As David said to Ahimelech, it needs to be said to the church today: "The king's business required haste" (I Samuel 21:8). What we do, we must do quickly!

CLOCK OF LIFE

The clock of life is wound but once,
And no man has the power
To say just when the hands will stop;
At late, or early hour.

Now is the only time we own
To do His precious will,
Do not wait until tomorrow;
For the clock may then be still.

God has given the church this hour of time. No one asked to be born during this era of time, but born we were for such a time as this. God has a divine will for each individual as well as the church. We must use the time He has given us wisely.

Remember, "Each moment is the meeting place of two eternities."

WE ARE AT THE END

Prophetically we are in the end time. Where are we on God's calendar?

The setting is right for harvest. The last several years, we have noticed an increase in the momentum of revival until we are seeing a great receptivity by the people throughout the world. There are many contributing factors to the harvest being ready. I bring to you an analogy again of the farmer. We know there are a number of ingredients involved in preparing the grain for harvest: sunshine and rain and then more sunshine and rain. But the closer we arrive to the harvest, it would appear that there is more sunshine. Nature itself has provided a means whereby the grain or the crop would be ripe and ready unto harvest. Likewise, God Almighty has prepared the necessary elements and ingredients to prepare men and women's hearts for this rapid harvest at the end time. We know according to Scripture, that men can come to the Lord only if the Spirit of the Lord draws them. For this reason, God's Spirit is working throughout the earth to prepare the hearts of men and women. All the necessary ingredients that are apparent in our world and universe are definitely related to the hand of God.

There is another factor involved. We are in a transitional time. We recognize that the door is soon to be closed on the Gentiles. The great outpouring of the Spirit that has been manifested for 2,000 years, which we refer to as the Church Dispensation or the Grace Dispensation, is soon to close as the fullness of the Gentiles is at hand. Then God will turn back and deal with Israel as a nation. As this door is nearing a period of closing, the Lord has prepared the hearts of men and women for a mighty ingathering into the kingdom of God in this final hour. Most all theologians that understand the prophetical teaching of the Bible are quick to acknowledge the church is near to reaching the point of rapture. Indeed the harvest is ripe.

"And it came to pass, that when all our enemies heard thereof, and all the heathen that were about us saw these things, they were much cast down in their own eyes: for they perceived that this work was wrought of our God."

Nehemiah 6:16

CHAPTER SEVEN

THE SUPERNATURAL

We are brothers and sisters of like precious faith. This movement must be filled with much love and appreciation for one another. Jesus said, "By this shall all men know that ye are my disciples, if ye have love one to another" (John 13:35). We share a profound revelatory truth that our forefathers were greatly despised for and it is not shared by the religious world of tradition, for it is anchored in the Word of God: the Mighty God in Christ Jesus and baptism in His name!

Many of us have come out from traditional Christianity and now we are going to propagate this truth all over the world. This can only happen if we are bonded together with love. We have only one Lord and King! There should be no big and little or important and non-important people among us. I want to make it perfectly clear that we as God's people, who make up the church, are all of great importance. I want to hear your thoughts or opinions whether you are an older or younger minister. We are brothers and sisters: young, middle-aged and old, with different personalities and gifts, but ONE BODY, ONE CHURCH and ONE MESSAGE for ONE WORLD that Jesus died for. We have ONE VISION: to bring the gospel to every person. What an awesome task!

It is the business of Satan to keep us from fulfilling this mission. If he can ever divide us, he will succeed. He will try to get us to major on our differences rather than our common bond of truth, but we have much more in common than the things that divide us.

As your general superintendent, I have asked God to help me to lead this great movement into this latter day harvest. The preaching of the gospel of Jesus Christ must be accompanied by the *supernatural acts of God*, and by the spirit of true holiness.

Where does the supernatural come from or begin? It all starts with the power of God; therefore, the church must get in contact with God as never before. This is done through prayer and meditating on His Word.

When the disciples were unable to operate in the realm of the supernatural, they asked Jesus why. Jesus answered them in Mark 9:29: "And he said unto them, This kind can come forth by nothing, but by prayer and fasting." *By nothing, but by prayer and fasting.*

PRAYER

Without prayer the church will dry up in the spirit; they will refuse to give themselves, their time or the finances to further the gospel. It is prayer that gives people the inspiration to go beyond themselves. Jesus gave a warning concerning the last days in Luke 21:34-36: "And take heed to yourselves, lest at any time your hearts be overcharged with surfeiting, and drunkenness, and cares of this life, and so that day come upon you unawares. For as a snare shall it come on all them that dwell on the face of the whole earth. Watch ye therefore, and pray always, that ye may be accounted worthy to escape all these things that shall come to pass, and to stand before the Son of man."

Jesus gave the answer on how the church can be alert and ready for His coming: WATCH and PRAY ALWAYS!

Programs are good and necessary but NOTHING can take the place of prayer! Jesus declared in Luke 18:1:

"Men ought ALWAYS to PRAY, and not to faint."

There is the word "always" again. In 2002 I am asking the pastor of every church, whether small or large, of the UPCI to organize a daily or weekly prayer group on a

> It is imperative for the church to watch and PRAY always!

consistent basis to pray that the Lord of the harvest would send forth laborers into the harvest field that is ripe. Think of the power that will be generated.

"And when they had prayed, the place was shaken where they were assembled together;

and they were all filled with the Holy Ghost,
and they spake the word of God
with boldness."
Acts 4:31

We already have the powerful Network of Prayer that is reaching around the world, and everyone should become a part of this. *Every* church should plug into the Network of Prayer. I encourage the women to be involved in the powerful Daughters of Zion network of prayer, which is already in many nations. This is the time to get involved and pray as Jesus instructed us to do!

FASTING

When James was giving instructions to the church on how to overcome worldliness, he wrote: "Be afflicted, and mourn, and weep. . . . Humble yourselves in the sight of the Lord, and he shall lift you up" (James 4:9-10).

How do people afflict themselves? It is not in the cutting of the flesh; it is in the humbling of the soul. Ezra proclaimed a fast at the river of Ahava, ". . . that we might AFFLICT ourselves before our God, to seek of Him a right way for us, and for our little ones, and for all our substance" (Ezra 8:21). WE AFFLICT OURSELVES TO SEEK HIM.

"The hand of our God is upon all them for good that seek him; but his power and his wrath is against all them that forsake him. So we FASTED and besought our God for this: and he was intreated of us" (Ezra 8:22-23).

Seeking God is done through PRAYER, FASTING, and studying the WORD. The men and women of the Old Testament knew that when prayer was accompanied with fasting, something happened.

When Jehoshaphat, king over Judah, was surrounded by enemies, Jehoshaphat proclaimed a FAST throughout all Judah. "And Jehoshaphat feared, and set himself to seek the LORD, and proclaimed a fast throughout all Judah. And Judah gathered themselves together, to ask help of the LORD" (II Chronicles 20:3-4).

They not only sought the Lord through prayer and fasting, but God spoke to them and gave them instructions how to win the battle against their enemies.

The Old Testament is filled with examples of those who sought the Lord through prayer and fasting. Jesus also gave instructions on fasting, and the early church followed His example and direction.

Jesus assumed they would fast and told them how to fast in Matthew 6:16: "Moreover when ye fast, be not, as the hypocrites, of a sad countenance: for they disfigure their faces, That they may appear unto men to fast. Verily I say unto you, They have their reward. But thou, when thou fastest, anoint thine head, and wash thy face; That thou appear not unto men to fast, but unto thy Father which is in secret: and thy Father, which seeth in secret, shall reward thee openly."

Fasting is not to be done to impress people or show how spiritual one is, but it is important in humbling oneself in seeking after God.

There is a dimension in the Spirit that can only be attained when prayer is coupled with fasting. Jesus referred to this in Mark 9:29: "And he said unto them, This kind can come forth by nothing, but by prayer and fasting."

Jesus was the great example in preparing for His ministry. He fasted forty days and nights. He never would have practiced anything that He did not want His followers to follow.

The early church practiced this in the Book of Acts. "And when they had fasted and prayed, and laid their hands on them, they sent them away" (Acts 13:3).

We do wrong when we think we can operate in the realm of the Spirit without following the practice of the early church. They PRAYED, FASTED, WITNESSED, DID MIRACLES and were full of ZEAL, proclaiming the GOSPEL OF JESUS CHRIST!

"So built we the wall;
and all the wall was joined
together unto the half
thereof: for the people
had a mind to work."

Nehemiah 4:6

CHAPTER EIGHT

MOBILIZATION

GROWTH

The facts are that other religions are growing and they are without truth; namely they are Mormons, Jehovah Witnesses, and the Islam religion.

The Mormons have thousands of young people going out all over the earth to full-time missionary work. They give two years of their life.

In order for a Jehovah Witness to receive special recognition in the life to come they must spend so many hours a day in witnessing.

Islam has become one of the fastest growing religions because of their fervent zeal and evangelistic thrust.

The fact is that the Mormons do not have this precious truth of the Holy Scriptures. The Muslims do not know the true eternal God, Jesus Christ. Many other Christian religions do not understand the whole gospel of Jesus Christ. We have the truth of who Jesus is, but we need a revolution in our concepts how to evangelize this ONE WORLD!

We emphasize the name of Jesus in baptism, and one God and that Jesus is His name. We do have a message that sets us apart from other growing religions, but our message is the message that Jesus set forth for His disciples to speak and teach. This message must burn in the hearts of our young people, the children, the ministers, the saints, and all those who are called according to His purpose.

MOBILIZING THE FORCES

It is necessary for all pastors to mobilize the people of their congregation. A mighty army is inactive, sitting on the pews of our churches. If the people are ever awakened to who they really are in Christ, the church would experience a great revolution, and would shake the gates of hell. This army, thus released from apathy and tradition, would conquer and destroy the strongholds of its enemy.

The late Reverend James Dallas shared with me a story of something that happened in Great Britain several years ago. He and his wife were in a restaurant and there was a group of Islam girls who kept looking their way. Finally one of them came over to them and asked, "Do you remember me, Brother Dallas?" He was taken aback when she called his name, for only her eyes were showing under the heavy veil which she wore on her face. She went on to say that she used to go to their church, but had been converted to the Islamic religion.

The cry is that the FIRE of the Holy Ghost must burn so mightily within our churches that no one would want to leave the truth and go into such false doctrine. The FIRE in our spirit must match the mighty doctrine of truth!

The church must be mobilized into a mighty army marching forward towards any and all false doctrine and not flinch, but stand true and strong in the face of all opposition and alluring doctrines of false peace. We have the true PRINCE OF PEACE, and we must tell the world about Him.

HOLY GHOST FIRE

Luke 3:16 states, "John answered, saying unto them all, I indeed baptize you with water; but one mightier than I cometh, the latchet of whose shoes I am not worthy to unloose: he shall baptize you with the Holy Ghost and with fire."

Many commentaries state that the early church fathers believed and taught that the Holy Ghost and FIRE was associated with the outpouring of the Spirit on the Day of Pentecost; others feel this FIRE is for purification and judgment only. Matthew Henry wrote the following:

> *They who are baptized with the Holy Ghost are baptized as with fire; the seven spirits of God appear as seven lamps of fire, Rev. 4.5. Is fire*

enlightening? So the Spirit is a Spirit of illumination. Is it warming? And do not their hearts burn within them? Is it consuming? And does not the Spirit of judgment, as a Spirit of burning, consume the dross of their corruptions? Does fire make all it seizes like itself? And does it move upwards? So does the Spirit make the soul holy like itself, and its tendency is heaven-ward.

Clarke's Commentary explains the phrase, "*With the Holy Ghost, and with fire*" thusly: "Christ's religion was to be a spiritual religion, and was to have its seat in the heart. This was the province of the Spirit of God, and of it alone; therefore He is represented here under the similitude of *fire*, because He was to *illuminate* and *invigorate* the soul, and *penetrate* every part."

We preach Holy Ghost with tongues, but little emphasis on the FIRE. It was the FIRE that was to illuminate, invigorate, and penetrate into the very core of a person. The FIRE of God is powerful!

If we can get the FIRE in every saint, the devil cannot stop the momentum of the church. We need to be immersed in the FIRE!

WORKERS TOGETHER

The cry of the workers under Nehemiah's direction was: "Let us rise up and build. So they strengthened their hands for this good work" (Nehemiah 2:18). Paul gives the same message to the church in II Corinthians 6:1: "We then, as workers together with him, . . ." We are WORKERS TOGETHER WITH HIM!

In 2002, we must organize our forces from the least

104

to the greatest. Our elderly, our youth, the children, and the middle-aged need to be trained to teach home Bible studies. There was a time when our churches were much more heavily into busing people to church. Maybe we need to take another look at this. We must get our people to take it to the streets. If we keep it in the building, the world will never be saved.

Each pastor needs to sit down with the leaders of his church and plan their strategy. It would be good for each church to have a commitment service early on in the year 2002 and put forth a strong effort to get every child of God to commit to reach the lost.

The story is told of a little girl who wandered away from her home in the country of the Canadian plains. All around the farm as far as the eye could see was the ripened golden grain.

When it was discovered that she was missing, her mother called her name again and again, but there was no response, for the child had wandered out somewhere in the fields and was lost to the call of her mother.

Frantically the mother and father searched and soon neighbors had come to help and yet they could not find her. The evening shadows were gathering and they feared the cold of the night would claim the life of their daughter.

As the news spread, the farming community and others joined in the search. The hours were passing and through the night they searched until someone suggested a more effective way of finding the lost child would be to join hands.

As the long line of some ninety searchers spread out and combed the field, a cry was lifted from one of the searchers, "Here she is!" When the frantic mother and father ran to where the child was they looked into the sightless eyes of their darling little girl. Death had claimed her by the exposure of the night. The mother cried out these words: "Would to God we would have joined hands sooner!"

The night is far spent, the lost are dying, and it is time for the church to join hands in their effort to reach the lost before it is too late. Let us join hands NOW, as never before, so the Master does not have to cry, "Would to God they had joined hands sooner!"

"So neither I, nor my brethren, nor my servants, nor the men of the guard which followed me, none of us put off our clothes, saving that every one put them off for washing."

Nehemiah 4:23

CHAPTER NINE

SELF-DISCIPLINE

The work of God must become the most important thing in our life. There was once a young communist lad standing on a street corner handing out communist propaganda. His clothes were tattered and torn, and a man passing by said to him, "You're paying a great price to spread your doctrine."

The young lad answered, "No price is too great when you're changing the world."

For the early church, the work of God became the most important thing in their life. They were racing with time and could not afford to be distracted from their purpose.

Paul states in I Corinthians 9:27: "But I keep under my body, and bring it into subjection: lest that by any means, when I have preached to others, I myself should be a castaway." Scofield commentary: "buffet my body, and lead it captive."

The greatest test of a man's character is how he takes charge of his own life.

SELF DENIAL

"If any man will come after me, let him deny himself, and take up his cross, and follow me" (Matthew 16:24). DENY HIMSELF!

A soldier of the cross is much like a soldier in the army. Anyone who serves their country in the military will find that there are two things required: Submission to authority and self-discipline.

Self-denial is putting Christ in first place instead of self. "A Christian is a mind through which Christ thinks; a heart through which Christ loves; a voice through which Christ speaks; a hand through which Christ helps."

Jack R. Taylor explains what staying dead to self means: "There is no other way to overcome the self-life than through the work of the Holy Spirit constantly applying the meaning of the cross. Without the constant work of the Holy Spirit filling our lives with Himself, we are forever 'stirring in the coffin.' Our constant consent to His constant application of the deeper meaning of the cross keeps us in the *position of death* that we might constantly know the *power of His Life.*"

DISCIPLINE OF THE MIND

How we think determines our performance. If you think you can, you will. Performance, good or bad, will be determined by attitude. Those who have received the power of the Holy Spirit have Jesus Christ dwelling inside; thus everything Jesus represents: salvation, power to witness, casting out demons, overcoming sin, pulling down strongholds of Satan, etc., they can do through Him. Paul said it in Philippians 4:13: "I can do all things through Christ which strengtheneth me."

Vision, looking beyond the common place, finds new things to do. And growth, as it always must, follows where mind marks the way.

The mind can never be chained. It is up to the individual to order its thoughts. John Bunyan was shut up in a Bedford jail that he might not preach the gospel. His tireless soul refused to be enchained. He wrote what was for centuries the most popular book written in the English language, *Pilgrim's Progress.*

Paul himself, when a prisoner at Rome was chafing because he could not go and preach to the churches, wrote letters which have been preached to all generations since.

> *Your disposition will be suitable to that which you most frequently think on; for the soul is, as it were, tinged with the color and complexion of its own thoughts.*
>
> —MARCUS AURELIUS

BEYOND THE VISION

The journey between the vision and the fulfillment of the vision are two different things. When Jesus talked to

111

His disciples about His kingdom, they could not see Gethsemane and Calvary. When Jesus said, "Follow me," they did not see the suffering that would be theirs.

When Moses instructed the children of Israel about leaving Egypt, all they could see was the deliverance. They could not see the Red Sea they would face.

Joseph had a vision of his brothers bowing down before him while he was in a leadership position. He did not see the pit, the foreign land, the lies, and the prison.

Each of the disciples and the apostles did not realize when they put their name on the dotted line to follow Christ that their life would end in martyrdom or that they would suffer great persecution. They were called to seal their doctrines with their blood, as the following facts will attest:

Matthew suffered martyrdom by being slain with a sword at a distant city of Ethiopia.

Mark expired at Alexandria, after being cruelly dragged through the streets of that city.

Luke was hanged upon an olive tree in the classic land of Greece.

John was put in a caldron of boiling oil, but escaped death in a miraculous manner, and was afterward banished to Patmos.

Peter was crucified at Rome with his head downward.

James, the Greater, was beheaded at Jerusalem.

James, the Less, was thrown from a lofty pinnacle of the temple, and then beaten to death with a fuller's club.

Bartholomew was flayed alive.

Andrew was bound to a cross, whence he preached to his persecutors, until he died.

Thomas was run through the body with a lance at Coromandel in the East Indies.

Jude was shot to death with arrows.

Matthias was first stoned and then beheaded.

Barnabas of the Gentiles was stoned to death at Salonica.

Paul, after various tortures and persecutions, was at length beheaded at Rome by the Emperor Nero.

As these great men gave their lives for the gospel of Jesus Christ; may the church do the same in word and in deed as the following poem describes:

CHRIST HAS NO HANDS

Christ has no hands but our hands to do His work today

He has no feet but our feet to lead men in the way

He has no tongue but our tongue to tell men how He died

He has no help but our help to bring them to His side.

We are the only Bible the careless world will read.

We are the sinner's gospel; we are the scoffer's creed;

We are the Lord's last message, given in word and deed;

What if the type is crooked? What if the print is blurred?

What if our hands are busy with other work than His?

What if our feet are walking where sin's

allurement is?
What if our tongue is speaking of things His
lips would spurn?
How can we hope to help Him or welcome
His return?

—ANNIE JOHNSTON FLINT

"And I looked, and rose up, and said unto the nobles, and to the rulers, and to the rest of the people, Be not ye afraid of them: remember the Lord, which is great and terrible, and fight for your brethren, your sons, and your daughters, your wives, and your houses."

Nehemiah 4:14

CHAPTER TEN

RELATIONSHIPS

"Love knows no limit to its endurance, no end to its trust, no fading of its hope; it can outlast anything. It is, in fact, the one thing that still stands when all else has fallen."

—I Corinthians 13:7-8

(J.B. Phillips, *Letters to Young Churches*)

LOVE FOR ONE ANOTHER

"A new commandment I give unto you, That ye love one another; as I have loved you, that ye also love one another" (John 13:34).

We cannot be bickering and fighting with one another.

I John 4:7 states: "Beloved, let us love one another: for love is of God; and every one that loveth is born of God, and knoweth God." It is imperative to learn to get along and try to understand one another.

Paul explained that if we could do miracles and have not love, it would all be in vain. The highest plateau in God's kingdom is learning to love as God loves. True love is where miracles take place.

We cannot accomplish God's vision and purpose with schism and strife in the body. We have many differences of opinions that have nothing to do with our doctrine. Our cause of reaching the world is far greater than our differences.

Peter and Paul had differences over circumcism, but they did not let it hinder them from doing all they could to further the gospel of Jesus Christ.

Love is not blind—it sees more, not less. But because it sees more, it is willing to see less.
—RABBI JULIUS GORDON

PASTOR AND CHURCH

It is significant that Jesus is referred to as the "chief Shepherd" (I Peter 5:4). The implication is very clear. Because He is Chief, pastors are under shepherds. They must get their instructions and inspiration from Him, and in the end they will give an account to Him for their life's work.

Ephesians 4:11 states that God gives pastors. They are the recognized "shepherds" of the flock. The pastor is a shepherd not a hireling. The shepherd fights the wolf, but the hireling will flee when the wolf comes. The hireling is busy doing too many other things that are more important to him than his sheep. The flock must be preserved from wolves and the doctrine kept sound and untarnished. The shepherd must fight the wolf of worldliness and false doctrine. We do not gain anything by evading the issues. We must protect the flock! We must not only protect them, but also feed the flock. A flock well-fed is least likely to become unhealthy spiritually or to get into trouble.

The "sheep" will follow the shepherd's voice. The responsibility of the pastor is great, but every need can be met through the oversight of the Chief Shepherd. It is important for the under shepherd to keep in close contact with the Chief Shepherd, because the sheep follow so closely.

> A minister wisely observed: "A pastor is the servant of the people, but they are not his master. There is only one who is his Master, even the Lord Jesus Christ."

I am asking every pastor to live on the cutting edge, to adopt the lifestyle of the early church in the form of their passion, sacrifice, prayer life, and fervency. God will guide the pastor, and he must recognize the importance of the "checks" of the Holy Spirit as well as the "promptings."

It is important to keep the vision before the church, to keep the people focused on the mission of the church and the great commission of Christ.

ACCOUNTABILITY

As men and women of God we all need to be accountable to someone. This is a protection to our ministry. There have been far too many casualties in the ministry. While the ministry is a call from Almighty God, we are still very human, and in our humanity very vulnerable to the temptations of the flesh, but by each minister becoming accountable to someone, we help protect one another. We should say to someone we respect, "If you ever see me do anything, say anything or go anywhere that would jeopardize my ministry, which is the highest call, please care about me enough to warn me or talk to me about it."

> **It is time to catch the vision!**
> ONE GOD
> ONE WORLD
> ONE MESSAGE
> ONE VISION
> Reach the world
> with the gospel
> of Jesus Christ!

We cannot afford to lose men needlessly in this end-time army!

Not only should we be accountable to one another, but more importantly, there must be an awareness of accountability to God. Paul stated, "We labour, that, whether present or absent, we may be accepted of him. For we must all appear before the judgment seat of Christ" (II Corinthians 5:9-10). The purpose for appearing before the judgment seat of Christ is not to determine the question of salvation, but the quality of service for the Master.

Do all the good you can, by all the means you can, in all the ways you can, in all the places you can, at all the times you can, to all the people you can and as long as you can.

—JOHN WESLEY

EPILOGUE

The vision must be structured. Successful leaders plan ahead. I ask each pastor or assigned church leaders to seek the face of God for this year, 2002. Then plan and make it the most effective year of your ministry. Take the following calendar and fill it in with events as God leads you. Then make sure to follow the plan each day and make the vision become a reality.

We must plan for prayer meetings, revivals, outreach, commitment service for the whole church, mission service, home Bible study rallies, etc. "Plan your work and work your plan."

January 2002

S	M	T	W	T	F	S
		1	2	3	4	5
6	7	8	9	10	11	12
13	14	15	16	17	18	19
20	21	22	23	24	25	26
27	28	29	30	31		

February 2002

S	M	T	W	T	F	S
					1	2
3	4	5	6	7	8	9
10	11	12	13	14	15	16
17	18	19	20	21	22	23
24	25	26	27	28		

March 2002

S	M	T	W	T	F	S
					1	2
3	4	5	6	7	8	9
10	11	12	13	14	15	16
17	18	19	20	21	22	23
24 / 31	25	26	27	28	29	30

April 2002

S	M	T	W	T	F	S
	1	2	3	4	5	6
7	8	9	10	11	12	13
14	15	16	17	18	19	20
21	22	23	24	25	26	27
28	29	30				

May 2002

S	M	T	W	T	F	S
			1	2	3	4
5	6	7	8	9	10	11
12	13	14	15	16	17	18
19	20	21	22	23	24	25
26	27	28	29	30	31	

June 2002

S	M	T	W	T	F	S
						1
2	3	4	5	6	7	8
9	10	11	12	13	14	15
16	17	18	19	20	21	22
23 / 30	24	25	26	27	28	29

July 2002

S	M	T	W	T	F	S
	1	2	3	4	5	6
7	8	9	10	11	12	13
14	15	16	17	18	19	20
21	22	23	24	25	26	27
28	29	30	31			

August 2002

S	M	T	W	T	F	S
				1	2	3
4	5	6	7	8	9	10
11	12	13	14	15	16	17
18	19	20	21	22	23	24
25	26	27	28	29	30	31

September 2002

S	M	T	W	T	F	S
1	2	3	4	5	6	7
8	9	10	11	12	13	14
15	16	17	18	19	20	21
22	23	24	25	26	27	28
29	30					

October 2002

S	M	T	W	T	F	S
		1	2	3	4	5
6	7	8	9	10	11	12
13	14	15	16	17	18	19
20	21	22	23	24	25	26
27	28	29	30	31		

November 2002

S	M	T	W	T	F	S
					1	2
3	4	5	6	7	8	9
10	11	12	13	14	15	16
17	18	19	20	21	22	23
24	25	26	27	28	29	30